NOVELTY AS CRITERIA OF PATENT IN INDIA

VOLUME 2, ISSUE 3 OF BRILLOPEDIA

DR. PRAHALAD AND MR. SANJEEV NIMESH

Contents

Preface

"Start writing, no matter what. The water does not flow until the faucet is turned on".

-Louis L'Amour

Hundreds of students and professors are contributing their work to Brillopedia, we are here to provide ample information about Law and Contemporary issues. Our aim is to provide a platform for today's generation to express their views and ideas on law and contemporary law.

Author

Dr.Prahalad

Publication

This research paper is published in volume 2, issue 3 of Brillopedia

CHAPTER ONE

ABSTRACT

According to Kalyan C. Kankanala, "A patent is not a licence to generate money; it is a licence to stop everyone else from getting profit." To determine if an invention submitted for patenting is new, the concept of novelty is employed as a guiding principle. The essay is broken down into three portions after an introductory by the author.

The author briefly examined the 3 trials and the notion of novelty in India in first group's discussion of "novelty as criterion of patentable subject matter in India." The notion of novelty in the U.K. and the U.S. is briefly explored in chapter two's discussion of "novelty as criterion of patentable subject matter in U.K. & U.S." Existing research in chapter 3, where he discusses "parallels and differences in the patent structure of India, U.K., & U.S.," where he briefly discusses how the patent systems in these nations operate in terms of their differences and similarities. The article has been finished by the author.

KEYWORDS-Introduction, Patents Law in India, Patent system in U.S, Comparative analysis, Patent system concepts, similarities and dissimilarities

CHAPTER TWO

INTRODUCTION

Patents are rights given in relation to innovations, or technology advances, large and little, that demonstrate at minimum a sliver of creativity over the state of the art.[1] According to the utilitarian perspective, if a procedure or commodity is made widely available to the public, more people will utilise it in application and encourage the community to even further improve it, which in turn will lead to clarity, the creator benefits commercially and exclusively from a new discovery. Despite the appearance of a major victory, there is a weakness that still exists. of scavengers. Consequently, there may be instances where the innovation is used without

Another negative aspect of economic oppression is that it could tempt people to file patent applications for trivial items, insignificant breakthroughs, even background knowledge, etc.

Nevertheless, the abovementioned effects and their remedies are reflected in the regulations of different countries has resulted of adequate legislation on intellectual property. In all patent regimes, to varying levels of severity, the fundamental concepts of patentability, novelty, and definiteness of patentability all, in fact, shared.[2] This article's main goal is to provide readers with a comprehensive understanding of the legal equality across various nations so they may make an educated judgement about whether to file for a patent.

A condition of stagnation could develop from more development.

A patent is often a restrictive right that grants the holder the sole right to exploit the invention for business reasons. The innovation cannot be used or sold commercially, though, according to the patent. A further clearance for selling will be given. Thus, patents are a legitimate way to impose a franchise agreement and unfair methods of competition. The monopolistic limitation time strives to encourage invention while also fairly balancing the interests of community and the interests of the person. This should be mentioned that patent disputes serve to ensure the essential growth in manufacturing, sales, and research and development as well as to encourage innovation. However, patent law, as part of the conventional intellectual schemes which has a great local roots and is in compliance with different national legislations.

Three key requirements—novelty, important concept, and industrial applicability—must be met for an innovation to qualify for patent rights. The current previous art in a specific technology generally determines the novelty component of a given innovation. The word "prior artwork" relates to already-known information which is in the public realm and encompasses periodicals, current goods, and every other type of open communication in the concerned sector.

"A new model or procedure containing an invention and industrial applicability use," according to the Indian Patent Act of 1970, is what is meant by "innovation." Therefore, one requirement for determining an invention's qualification for a patents is novelty.

According to Section 2(i)l of the Indian Patents Act, 1970, "any innovation or techniques that has not been predicted by publishing in any report to be used in the nation or somewhere else in the planet well before time of submission of patent application with prescribed form, i.e. the source matcrial has not gone down into public realm or that this does not appear to be part of the state of art," is considered to be a "modern innovation." If a new innovation cannot be explained by a former publishing, prior public knowledge, or even a prior application, it is said to be novel.

An invention is new if it has not been disclosed in the prior art where the prior art means everything that has been published, presented or otherwise disclosed to the public even before the date of filing of specification.

Novelty should always be ascertained with reference to a single prior art reference. It means that all features of the subject invention should be present in a single document such that each and every novel element of the alleged claim should be disclosed in the prior art document. Various documents cannot be combined to determine novelty of a particular invention, instead various documents when combined together decides on the inventive step.

Although, the patent act does not define the phrase "State of art". In such kind of situations, it is to be ascertained from the interpretation given by the court.

The primary factors that determine whether a subject is eligible for patent protection are novelty and industrial application. The distinction between innovation and finding can be seen in novelty. This distinction has been present in the US for years in the "product of environment theory" and other related phrases.

"Bio-patents" are the term used to describe patents that are awarded to biological things. Varying nations have different patenting restrictions on living things. New life patents, however, are founded on distinctions between new life and recognised substances in terms of their qualities and uses because the conventional criteria of novelty and non-obviousness equally apply to living matter. Whether that is necessary to capture a patent solely by removing genes and microbes from their natural habitat differs from nation to nation.

For instance, if the invention satisfies the legislative requirements for patentable subject matter, a "cleansed and isolated" substance is regarded as a patentable topic in the United States. Gene patents, though, only apply to isolated and pure genes; they do not protect naturally produced genes. The European Union, however, states that "biological molecules extracted from the natural surroundings or manufactured by technical procedures could be the object of the innovation, even if they had been implementation framework in environment." The criteria for issuing patents on living organisms clearly makes this a difficult and frequently contentious matter.

[1]Intellectual Property: Patents, Copyrights, Trademarks and allied rights, (5th ed. 2003)

[2]J.W. Baxter: Patent Law and Practice, Ed. 1968, pp.73.

CHAPTER THREE

PATENT LAW IN INDIA

According to the Indian Patent Act of 1970, merely discovering a new use for an existing compound or its modern version does not qualify as a patentable invention.[1] Article 27 of the TRIPS Agreement states that, "Pursuant to the clauses of paragraphs two and three, patents must therefore be accessible for any creations, as to if product lines or procedures, in all technological fields, supplied that they too are fresh, require an original creation, and are competent of embedded device,"[2] that also suggests that India, as a TRIPS Agreement group, explicitly integrates the "Patentable Subject Matter" into its legal provisions.

It's been emphasised again and again that the simple finding of a unique conception of a known material docs not increase the effectiveness of that material, unless known mechanism develops a new output or uses at minimum one new ingredient.[3]

The term "patent" refers to a privilege given to anybody who creates a novel and valuable procedure, item, piece of production, properties of the materials, or any novel and practicalenhancement of any such thing.[4]The goal of patent policy is to encourage latest tech, industrial activities, and science and research.[5]

A novel item or procedure incorporating an original creation and suitable for commercial use is referred to as a "innovation."[6] Even a process involving an original creation constitutes an innovation inside the purview of the Law, as is evident from a cursory reading of the language. Thus, it is not required that the successfully validated be an altogether fresh item. A thing would've been considered an innovation even if it underwent a significant improvement thanks to a patentability.[7] It should be emphasised that patents are granted for "inventions" as specified by the Patents Act of 1970 as well as "new discoveries."

The Apex Court made the following statement in the matter of ***Bishwananth Prasad RadheyShyam v. Hindustan Metal Industries***: "The underlying principle of Patent Law would be that a patent is given exclusively for an invention." This is fresh and beneficial.[8]

A finding should be differentiated from an innovation. But it has and always will be a concept.

simple findings or concepts really aren't patentable under patent law, only findings which have a technological contributions or technological component.[9]

It is widely accepted that a simple idea cannot qualify for patent protection.[10]An concept or invention is therefore not patentable, according to the fundamentals of patents act. It does not fall under the category of earlier art or method. The concept or invention becomes patentable once it is used in practise. It results in patentability although if, as is commonly the case, the discovery's practicality has indeed been realized and declared.[11] A patentable innovation could emerge from a finding or a concept if you really can demonstrate to others how it might be used in a useful way.

It would be the situation although it is evident how the finding or concept can be put to use after it has been discovered. Ramayana's description of the idea of flying rocks is little more than a thought. Its practical implementation does not render it ineligible under section 3 of the Patent Act of 1970.

A technical side of an innovation that differs from previous knowledge, has economic relevance, or even both, and renders it obscure to a person with normal ability in the field is said to have an original creation.[12] There must be a factors of production, financial relevance, or both in order to meet the innovative step. The notion that a patent might be issued based only on economic relevance weakened and undermined the need of technological improvements. [13]

In ***Dhanpat Seth v. Nilkamal Plastic Crates Ltd.***[14], the High court of Himachal Pradesh made the observation that an innovation need not be a completely new item; rather, it only needs to be vastly increased by an innovative technique.

In addition, Kitchin J. mentioned in ***Novartis AG v. Johnson & Johnson Medical Ltd.***[15] that it was necessary to demonstrate that now the prior art enclosed a clear explanation of, or specific directions to end up making, something which would unavoidably intrude the patentee's assertion if done just after grant of a patent in order to maintain for complete absence of novelty.

Additionally, the Apex Court of India in *M/S. Bishwanath Prasad RadheyShyam v. M/S Hindustan Metal Industries*[16] stated that this is crucial for an advancement on something recognised to be much more than a simple workbench advancement and should autonomously gratify the exam of discovery or a "opportunity for improvement" in sequence to be patentable.

[1]Commission of Intellectual Property Rights (CIPR) Report of September, 2002.

[2]Article 27, TRIPS Agreement

[3] Asian Electronics Ltd v. Havells India Limited 2010 (44) PTC66(Del)

[4]F.Hoffman-la Roche Ltd. V. Cipla Ltd, 2008 (37) P.T.C 71 (Del)

[5]Bishwananth Prasad RadheyShyam v. Hindustan Metal Industries, 1979 2 S.C.C. 511

[6]Section 2(1)(j), Patents Act, 1970

[7]Dhanpat Seth v. Nil Kamal Plastic Crates Ltd., 2008 (36) P.T.C 123 (H.P.) (DB)

[8]Bishwananth Prasad RadheyShyam v. Hindustan Metal Industries, (1979) 2 S.C.C 511.

[9]Hardwood v. Great Northern Railway Co., 11 H.L.C 654

[10]IBM Corp's Appln.(1980) F.S.R 568.

[11]Gale's Appln. (1991) R.P.C 305 (C.A)

[12]Section 2 (ja), Patents Act, 1970

[13]Ram NarainKher v. Ambassador Industries, New Delhi, A.I.R. 1976 Del 87.

[14](2008) 36 PTC 123 (HP)

[15]2009 EWHC 1671 (Pat)

[16]A.I.R 1982 SC 1444

CHAPTER FOUR

PATENT SYSTEM IN U.S

An innovative step should be taken in order for a patent to be valid. The Supreme Court of US established a number of criteria to be taken into account when determining whether or not an innovation was evident in the case of *Gragham v. John Deree Co.*[1]

1) the extent and substance of the patentability,

2) the distinctions between both the patent claims and an in question assertions, and

3) the degree of customary expertise in the relevant art. Additionally, the judges may take into account ancillary factors like

a) economic security,

b) long-felt demands that have not yet been met, and

c) other people's inability to find a solution.

The United States has consistently been the centre of patent battles, ranking among the first majority of industrialised countries, which led the majority of American-based businesses to adopt protective patenting strategies. In other terms, almost all of the businesses lacking an incentive to file a lawsuit. Other determining element is the high expense of lawsuit in the USA, where it is frequently believed that attorneys stand to gain the most from these conflicts. It has resulted in an unjustifiable rise in conflicts and lawsuits by speculation patent owners against corporations due to outmoded processes, resource scarcity, and antiquated regulations that burden the patent laws. The two most significant variables that have slowed technical advancement in the USA are rising legal fees and lawsuit anxiety.

Such variables that result in patent lawsuits are not factored into the equation by the U.S. Patent and Trademark Office (PTO). Within past 35 years, there have been 5 times quite so many patent applications as there were approvals due to the excessive quantity of low-quality patents[2].

The ability of a 3rd person to seek a re - examination of patents that have already been awarded is yet another legal element that enhances their legal disputes. In contrast to the strong "utility patent" of Japan and the EU, the opposition is given a set amount of time to voice concerns. When opposed to lawsuit, this is more effective and cost-effective.

Obama Signed a package of patent reform proposals in response to the growing issue of patent law suits and the annoyances they cause to many people. These initiatives are expected to transform the scheme into one that is far-reaching with lower legal expenses, enhance intellectual property quality, and foster creativity. "Patent trolls" are the focus of the changes. They are speculator who assert too broad patents, aggressively pursue suspected lawbreakers, take legal action, or agree to exorbitant licence payments. The SHIELD Act shields the sector from unfair and unwarranted lawsuits. On the other hand, the Leafy-Smith America Invents Act replaces the failed first to discover process with an innovator to file approach that's doing rid with interfering processes and after award resistance.

[1]Graham v. John Decree Co. 383 U.S 1 (1966)

[2]Toshiko Takenaka, Patent Law and Theory 391 (Edward Elgar Publications, 1st ed. 2008)

CHAPTER FIVE

COMPARATIVE ANALYSIS

Because they all provide innovators with specific rights for a specific amount of time in return for the revelation of the invention's production technique, the patent regimes of India, the US, and the UK appear to be very comparable. In addition, notwithstanding some local differences, their views on patentability, its repercussions, and its principal function in fostering innovation are strikingly similar. This, nevertheless, doesn't really fully capture the real picture of global patentability.We believe that there are significant distinctions between the European and American[1] patent systems, which are detailed in this article, despite the fact that famous experts have claimed that they are generally comparable.

The basic patent laws of the countries have ratified the European Patent Conventions are comparable to those of England, but the administrative legislation and court practices relating to patents are frequently considerably unlike. The latter leads to incomplete outcomes, as was seen in the well-known Remington v. Improver[2] case, in which the English and German tribunals reached different conclusions regarding violation. The balancing of probability analysis is the sort of evidence that the English courts take into account when determining whether patent should be deemed void.

[1]Peter Drahos, The Global Governance of Knowledge: Patent offices and their clients (2010)

[2](1990) FSR 181

CHAPTER SIX

PATENT SYSTEM CONCEPTS

Per se limitations of patentability depending only on the subject material of the innovation are typically in opposition to the core assumptions and motives of patent rights, according to a basic understanding of patented products.[1] By enabling the conversion of discoveries into brand-new services and goods, patent regimes spur innovation. [2]The provision of novel services and goods related to technological development[3] is the final advantage of patent systems for society and customers. Patents speed up the commercialisation process and allow inventors to profit from their efforts by limiting compctition' unauthorised use of the patented idea for a set amount of time.[4]

By doing this, the inventor may ensure a financially sound payback on the capital invested in turning the idea into a brand-new good or service.[5] Additionally, patent commonly used system that the innovations be fully disclosed in the issued patents' language.[6] Consequently, in contrast to a system that relies on proprietary information, patent programs promote the dissemination of knowledge for benefit to society. [7]

According to the suggested amendments to India's patent legislation, several types of subject material are not eligible for patent rights. Therefore, with the exception of per se individualcategories of subject material from the enrolment for patent rights, as the proposed changes to India's current patent suggestion, will indeed decrease

(1) the space for investment with regard to that subject material,

(2) the accessibility of new goods / services linked with just that subject material, and

(3) restrict the dissemination of information of scientific innovations. While Article 27 of the TRIPS Agreement gives WTO Members the option

excluding a select group of subject material from patentable subject matter, as is explained below, India's suggested omissions do not belong to this group.[8]

[1]See e.g., 35 U.S.C. § 101 (the United States Supreme Court has repeatedly and consistently stated that there

are only three categories of subject matter for which one may not obtain patent protection: (1) laws of

nature; (2) natural phenomena; and (3) abstract ideas).

[2]Commission on Intellectual Property Rights (CIPR), Integrating Intellectual Property Rights and Development Policy [hereinafter CIPR], available at http://www.iprcommission.org/papers/pdfs/final report/ CIPRfullfinal.pdf.

[3]David Encaoua, Dominique Gullec& Catalina Martinez, Patent systems for encouraging innovation:

Lessons from economic analysis (Feb. 2005),

[4]Id

[5]Id

[6]See e.g., 35 U.S.C. § 112.

[7]GauravWahie, Evaluating Trade Secrets Under The IPR Paradigm: The Hypothesis Of Trade Secrets As A

Right Analysed In The Pure Hohfeldian Sense,

[8]See TRIPS Agreement, supra note 1, art. 27. (providing that subject to the provisions of para. 2 and 3, patents shall be available for any inventions, whether products or processes, in all fields of technology, provided that they are new, involve an inventive step and are capable of industrial application and subject to para 4 of art. 65, para 8 of art. 70 and para.3 of this art., patents shall be available and patent rights enjoyable without, discrimination as to the place of invention, the field of technology and whether products are imported or locally produced).

CHAPTER SEVEN

OVERVIEW OF SIMPLE STANDARD FROMS OF PATENT LAWS

A variety of requirements are imposed by patent systems on people looking to secure a patent for an innovation. These requirements make guarantee that now the administration only grants patents when they are appropriate and also that the privileges given by the patent are commensurate with the creator's contributions. To evaluate whether the authorities may patent an idea, most patent regimcs apply three criteria:

1) the invention's uniqueness;

2) its innovative steps; and

3) its industrial applicability. These requirements are also reflected in the International Treaties.[1]A TRIP only outlines the conditions that an invention must satisfy in order to be eligible for patent protection; it makes no definition of what a "invention" is.[2]

TRIPS only outline the conditions that an innovation must satisfy in order to become eligible for patent protection; it makes no definition of what a "invention" is. Representatives have a great deal of latitude to define what an innovation is because of this uncertainty.[3] Additionally, as a mere discovery and not an invention, Member also may exclude it from patentability any material found naturally.

In addition to the three criteria listed above, the innovations must also satisfy the criteria for qualification and proper communication in order to be patentable.

[1]See Justine Pila, Bound Futures: Patent Law and Modern Biotechnology, 9(2) B.U.J. Sci. & Tech. Law

326, 378 (2003).

[2] See TRIPS Agreement, supra note 1, art. 27.1.

[3]Id

CHAPTER EIGHT

NOVELTY

The innovation must not have been previously known in the "prior art" in order to meet the novelty threshold (i.e., the whole of public accessed information which existed before the creator gives the patent request).[1] According to this condition, the data might not have been made public before to the user's initial submission date (the previous date).[2] "Under many approaches, material in available to the public formats (such as printed materials, inventions, demonstrated significant without restrictions and available with ordinary efforts) are included previous art."[3] WTO Members have the power to impose a requirement for a demonstration of innovation as a prerequisite to issuing a patent under TRIPS Article 27.1.[4]

Because a member only issues a patent whenever an innovator reveals anything novel, if the innovation is disclosed in material that is accessible to the general public, the petitioner (the "innovator") is not permitted to divulge anything novel in exchange for the award. The creator is not then eligible for a patent. In particular, the Members has the right to withdraw any patents which have already been awarded to the innovator.[5] The revelation could have happened locally or somewhere else from the globe. The finding of items which already occur in nature(such as a new facility or material) is not even an innovation because of the essence of innovation.[6]

[1]See, e.g., Convention on the Grant of European Patents art. 54 (2), Oct. 5, 1973, 1065 U.N.T.S. 255[hereinafter EPC],. (providing that the prior art shall include "everything made available to the public by means of a written or oral description, by use, or in any other way, before the date of filing of the European patent application.").

[2]European Patent Office (EPO) case law holds that the theoretical possibility of having access to information renders it available to the public (case T 444/88), whatever the means by which the invention was made accessible, and in the case of prior public use irrespective of whether

particular reasons exist for analyzing the product (cases G 1/92).

[3] See e.g., 35 U.S.C. § 102.
[4] See TRIPS Agreement, supra note 1, art. 27.1.
[5] See e.g., 35 U.S.C. § 102(b).
[6] See 35 U.S.C. § 102(a).

CHAPTER NINE

NOVELTY AS CRITERIAOFPATENTABILITY IN INDIA

According to the Patent Act of 1970, an item cannot be granted a patent in India just because a recognized material is being used in a novel way or in a unique conception. Article 27 of the TRIPS Agreement, which states that patents will be allowed for inventions in all technological fields, as to if products or procedures, has indeed been decided to add a stipulation that specifies that the innovation has to be innovative, have had an original creation, and also have a practical application. India is among the member nations which has agreed to sign the TRIPS Agreement as well as being a participant to this Contract.

Therefore, in India, an innovation must satisfy these three main criteria or standards in order to be represented as such.

The privilege awarded to someone who creates a novel and beneficial procedure, commodity, item, or substantiation a novel and beneficial modification thereof—is referred to as a patent. To assist the technological innovation, science and research, and industrial activities, patent legislation was introduced. An innovative stage is referred to as an innovation if it considerably enhances a business. Patents are issued in accordance with the Patent Act of 1970 for both "scientific breakthroughs" and "innovations" that demonstrate an innovative step.

We should make a distinction between creativity and finding, it is often remarked. Nevertheless, there really are rules governing patent system that state that fresh findings or concepts alone do not qualify as novel and innovative, and as a result, an item cannot be patented. On the other hand, it is asserted that even if the findings include continual improvement or specific technologies, the item will be patentable.

It is common knowledge that a patent cannot protect only conceptual inventions. Concepts and inventions cannot be so patented, according to the fundamentals of patents act. It is not considered to be a cutting-edge method or technology. Patentability can only result from the actual understanding of theories and findings. The practical implementation of the finding, if any, is patentable, as is frequently the case. Patentable innovations may result from the capacity to use findings and concepts to explain that they can be applied in significant ways. The Ramayana's description of rocks is merely an idea that a sacred epic explains. According to section 3 of the Patent Act, the exclusions is not triggered by the real use of it.[1]

Lack of novelty, often known as "expectation," is influenced by things like prior publications, commercially available goods, established titles and utilizations, and chosen innovations. The Patent Act does not define the term "anticipation," but it does contain provisions (S. 29 through S. 34) that help to determine what expectation is not. If the anticipating test reveals the existence of patent claims, the claim has been made if the prior art studies allow for the application of the patent application.Prior art assessment may not even need to be replicated, but employing the right skills, expert advice might be taken into consideration to help determine assumptions. Whether that is a pre requisite inside the claim, what is exhibited as a consequence of what is stated in the previous art can also be used to identify consistent outcomes.[2]

In India, the authorities will consider whether the innovation presented to them would be described in a patent or which other documentation has been published prior to filing when determining whether such a patent application is expected or not. The patent would not be awarded if it can be proved that it was existing; else, it will. If the creator who is applying for a patent can demonstrate that the innovation was released without his permission and that this was the case, then it cannot be stated that the claim is predicted. We can refer to the judgement given in *Lallubhai case*, and we can see that novelty is one of the important criteria in determining the patent eligibility as it is unknown and unused information that gives a competitive advantage to the inventor.

In the case of prior disclosure by the inventor, the Patent Act provides a one-year grace period for patent applications if the invention is described in front of an association of experts or published in the business of such an association of experts. The grace period can also be used to conduct appropriate investigations, such as for data for regulatory approval. Not available if the invention is commercially sold or processed in India.

Although it is not deemed premature in India, using or publishing the invention after submitting a preliminary patent application is. The following criteria, which are outlined under Sections 32, 31, and 3(p) respectively, will be taken into account as a substantial factor when evaluating novelty: publicly work, public presentation, and indigenous practices. It is also possible to anticipate inventions via expertise in local or indigenous societies in India or somewhere else, either verbal or not.

[1]Patent Act, 1970

[2] Novelty: An Indian Perspective, by PankajMusyuni (18 December 2017)

CHAPTER TEN

THREE-DIMENSIONAL APPROACH (Judicial Approach)

A patent application may be deemed foreseen in India under specific conditions, including when the innovation is described in a patent or another publication that was released earlier to the applicant's priority date. There are some exceptions to this revelation, though. For instance, if the creator can show that the information released was gained unlawfully from him because disclosed without his or her knowledge, the innovation is not regarded as expected.

In *LallubhaiChakubhaiJariwala v.ChimanlalChunilal and Co[1]* the tribunal stated that:

The two requirements for a patent's legality are originality and usefulness, but the invention's novelty stands as the true litmus test. Novelty is absolutely necessary because without it, the community would not receive any benefits, and as a result, the patentee would not be taken into account when determining what constitutes public usage and understanding.

The next issue would be whether the complainant's idea was foreseen by a previous user of the community, the court further stated. Does have the claimant or anyone else used this in publicly well before date of application? General user is a factual determination in every instance and does not refer to the general public using or exercising an innovation. The award would not be for a modern innovation or production if the innovation is being used before or at the time of the grant. This rule holds true whether patentee is using the innovation personally or by someone else.It has been ruled that the previous publicly sales of goods act or commodities handled according the innovation is a publicly utilisation innovation and that doing so constitutes a previous use that renders the patent worthless. The sales are definite evidence that the previous use was truly industrial and not exploratory.

As a result, anticipating applies to the invention's information release by any individual, such as the application, the creator, or the licensee. Any innovation loses its novelty if it is implemented and made available for purchase before the user's period of priority. Therefore, selling the goods before submitting a patent application is considered public knowledge.

[1]LallubhaiChakubhaiJariwala v. ChimanlalChunilal and Co

CHAPTER ELEVEN

GENERAL OBSERVATION ON STANDARD OF ANTICIPATION

By comparing an innovation, in any of its manifestations, with related equipment disclosed by (1) presenting evidence, or (2) public knowledge, novelty is assessed. Sections 29 to 34 of the Indian Patent Act specify the conditions in which an innovation is "regarded not to be foreseen," but the law is silent on how anticipating is determined.

- **Prior Publication**

Section 29 of the Act refers to prior art as that which was published before the claim of a completed specification in:

(i) any specification filed for obtaining a patent in India on or after January 1, 1912; (ii) in India or elsewhere and also in any other documents. The only exception is where the applicant can prove that the matter published was taken from him and published without his consent and that he had applied for the patent as soon as reasonably practicable after knowing about the publication. However, this exception will not be available where the invention has been commercially worked in India otherwise than for the purpose of reasonable trial.

In the *General Tire case*, Sachs LJ summarized the law on anticipation by prior publication as follows:

"It is essential to measure an older publishing with a patentee's claims in order to ascertain if the patentee's claims have indeed been foreseen by the previous publishing. The previous publishing must be understood for this reason as of the original publication, taking into account the pertinent environmental factors that existed previously, but without reference to future developments. In light of the underlying circumstances and conditions of release, the patentee's claims should be interpreted accordingly.The patentee's claims have indeed been foreseen, and not otherwise, if the previous article, when interpreted this way, reveals the identical device as the one the patent holder purports to have created in his claims. In such cases, the patentee is not really the genuine and original creator of the invention, and his patented invention is not fresh in accordance with section 32(1)(e) (this is equivalent to section 64(1)(e) of the Indian Patents Act).

- **Publicly Known/Use**

The phrase "commonly recognized or widely utilized" cannot be used to oppose a patent application. The importing of a manufactured product using the patented technology into India before to the relevant date would've been considered publicly known or public usage under explanatory section to s. 25(1)(d), unless it was done and for the purposes of a justifiable test or experimentation. Whereas the fact that the innovation is not novel is one of the reasons for revoking the patent under § 64(1)(e), consideration must also be given to what's been publicized in India or elsewhere though as what's been publicly known and used in India previous to the relevant date of the claim.

This section makes a distinction between what is generally believed or what is simply printed. Public knowledge cannot be established by simple publishing. But at the other hand, if something is widely used, it becomes known to the public even if it hasn't been written in a documentation.

The issue of public use and knowledge was examined by the Calcutta High Court in the case of ***Poysha Industries Ltd v. Deputy Controller of Patents and Designs.***[1]The innovation has either been publicly disclosed aware or been widely used in some region of India, according to the appellant' major argument to defend of their objection. It was asserted in support of this claim that since February 1960, M/s. Zandu Pharmaceuticals and then another business has purchased tin boxes with crimp diaphragms from the appellant. They argued that the claimant's method for crimped the lid of the box was standard and well-known in the business and didn't call for any special knowledge or abilities. The challenge, though, was unsuccessful because the appellants were unable to demonstrate that the invention was used and well recognised.

In ***Monsanto Co v. CoramandalIndag Products (P) Ltd.***,[2] it was held that:

"It is clear from the facts narrated by us that the Herbicide CP 53619 (Butachlor) was publicly known before Patent Number 125381 was granted. Its formula and use had already been made known to the public by the report of the International Rice Research Institute for the year 1968. No one claimed any patent or any other exclusive right in Butachlor. To satisfy the requirement of being publicly known as used in clauses (e) and (f) of [s 64(1)], it is not necessary that it should be widely used to the knowledge of the consumer public. It is sufficient if it is known to the persons who are engaged in the pursuit of knowledge of the patented product or process either as men of science or men of commerce or consumers. The section of the public who, as men of science or men of commerce, were interested in knowing about herbicides which would destroy weeds but not rice, must have been aware of the discovery of Butachlor. There was no secret about the active agent Butachlor as claimed by the plaintiffs since there was no patent for Butachlor, as admitted by the plaintiffs. Emulsification was the well-known and common process by which any herbicide could be used. Neither Butachlor nor the process of emulsification was capable of being claimed by the plaintiff as their exclusive property. The solvent and the emulsifier were not secrets and they were admittedly not secrets and they were ordinary market products. From the beginning to the end, there was no secret and there was no invention by the plaintiffs. The ingredients, the active ingredient, the solvent and the emulsifier, were known; the process was known, the product was known and the use was known. The plaintiffs were merely camouflaging a substance whose discovery was known throughout the world and trying to enfold it in their specification relating to Patent Number 125381. The patent is, therefore, liable to be revoked".

[1]AIR 1975 Cal 178

[2]AIR 1986 SC 712

CHAPTER TWELVE

THINGS THAT ARE NOT PATENTABLE

Section 3, 4 & 5 of the Patents Act, 1970

The main categories, which do not qualify for patentability under the IPA are:

- A creation whose application might be immoral or harmful to public order, or which gravely causes environmental pollution, the health of the people, animals, or plants. For instance, a novel kind of slot machine; atomic energy-related discoveries.
- This is the case since the Central Government is solely in charge of advancing atomic power, and it seems to reason that it wouldn't want patent rights to interfere with its plans.
- A frivolous innovation or one that makes claims that are blatantly at odds with well-known natural rules. A perpetual energy device claims, for instance, won't be eligible for patent protection because it will go against accepted universal forces.
- The simple statement of an abstract idea or the finding of a scientific law. For instance, a revelation just reveals something that was previously hidden; it does not entail an action that renders it valuable; as a result, it is not an innovation and cannot be patented. The creation of an abstract idea follows a similar logic. [S 3(d)
- A material created by simply mixing its constituent parts together, or a method for creating such a mixture;
- Merely arranging, rearranging, or duplicating existing equipment that all operate separately and in a known manner without altering the outcomes.
- A creation that effectively incorporates local traditions;

- An algorithm, computer software, or commercial or analytical technique.

Novartis AG v. Union of India and others (2007 Madras)

- Challenged the constitutionality of section 3(d), Violate of Article 14Not complied with TRIPS Agreement
- Regarding non-compliance, the court held that domestic court has no jurisdiction
- Held that 3(d) not violative of Article 14

Besides these rather obvious items the following items are also not inventions within the meaning of the Patents Act, as a matter of policy and are therefore, not patentable:

- A method of agriculture or horticulture;
- Any process for the medicinal, surgical, curative, prophylactic, diagnostic, therapeutic or other treatment of human beings and animals;
- Plants and animals in whole or part thereof other than micro-organisms;
- Seeds and biological processes for production of plants and animals;

The following two categories belong to different fields of intellectual property and are not subject matter of patents:

- A literary dramatic, musical or artistic work including cinematographic work and television productions (The Copyright Act);
- Topography of integrated circuits (The Semiconductor Integrated Circuits Layout- Design Act, 2000).

In the case of substances falling within certain categories no claim for patenting the substance can be entertained; however, claims for the methods or processes of manufacture of these substances can be patented. Such categories of substances are:

- Substances which could be used as food or medicine or drug;
- Substances prepared or produced by chemical processes (which include biochemical, biotechnological and microbiological process).

However, a claim for patenting a substance can be entertained if the substance itself is intended for use as medicine or drug – excepting chemical substances which are ordinarily used as intermediates in the preparation or manufacture of any medicines. Computer programmes and microorganisms have emerged as two special categories where patent protection is increasingly sought.

CHAPTER THIRTEEN

NOVELTY AS CRITERIA OF PATENTABILITY IN U. S & U.K

Anything like that could be produced (roughly) in the United States due to the demand for uniqueness. New technology is typically most dangerous when it originates from the creator or operator. This may unintentionally take place as presentation and proposals that are intended for a certain target are posted on the internet by several host organisations. After the inventor publishes their invention, there is indeed a one-year time limit in the US however during time patent applications can be made. Even though the creator makes this revelation after a year has passed, the novelty or clearness of the invention may be rejected based on public release. The majority of nations do not have a time limit, and articles are current as of the day of release.[1]

The US Supreme Court made various characteristics to take into account when figuring out is whether a discovery is noticeable in the Graham v. John Deere Co. case, including the comprehensiveness of the patent claims, the discrepancy between both the patent claims and the contested makes a claim, as well as the threshold of the normal individual talented in the technical knowledge. The decision also established that tribunals may employ secondary elements to judge that whether innovation is apparent by taking into account things like financial performance, long-term yet unmet requirements, and other people's incapacity to address the problem.

Patents cannot be issued in the United Kingdom for old innovations. The majority of other nations, including the UK, have quite strict standards for determining uniqueness. Any revelation, whether oral or written, made well before user's relevant date, anywhere else in the globe, may be detrimental to the patent filing. Maintaining the invention's secrecy up till it application has been submitted is crucial because prior publication might invalidate a provisional patent. That's not all, though. Despite appearing to be published, the innovation can still be patented.

[1] comparative analysis of patentability threshold in India, United States and United Kingdom, by DishaAdhikary, Amogh C. &ShwetaMallya

CHAPTER FOURTEEN

SIMILARITIES AND DISSIMILARITIES IN PATENT SYSTEM OF INDIA, U.K.& U.S.

In that they grant all creators particular rights for a fixed period of time in consideration for disclosing the invention's technique, the Indian, US, and UK patent regimes seem to be substantially comparable. Additionally, these three nations' approaches to patentability—which differs substantially from area to area but are essentially the same—play a significant role in fostering invention. This, though, will not provide a clear overview of global patentability. Several well-known academics contend that the European patent law and the US patent system are roughly equivalent, however I believe there are important differences between the two patented products.

Therefore, once we make comparisons the English patent system with the patent laws of the states that have signed the European Patent Convention, we could see that the substantiated patent system of these nations continue to stay the very same. However, there really are differences in the patent laws when we look at the legal customs and prescriptive laws of those nations. In Remington v. the Improver, a well-known current patent case wherein British and German courts were proven to have various approaches to violation, we can observe the differences between the patent laws of such two nations.

A British court uses a likelihood analysis to examine the evidence before considering to either cancelling a patent. To reject a patent that has already been awarded, though, requires clear and unambiguous proof in the US.

Between both the extensive and stringent US transparency laws and the European system, that does not need information unless particularly necessary, the UK courts have had some reporting requirements. Accordingly, the UK Discovery Rules require that you reveal the documents you are seeking as well as any others that may be relevant to your claim, other group's instance, or both.

From the perspective of who will obtain a patent for their idea earliest, other parallels and differences can be noted. Unlike the United States, where a patent is awarded to the individual who had first created it, the United Kingdom and India follow a new technique in which the patent is awarded to the individual who had first submitted for it, and under a first-to-invent scheme. If two people claim the very same discovery, the USPTO will decide the issue and determine who had the initial concept for the discovery.

From the perspective of the fixed term, more parallels and differences are apparent. The United Kingdom does not adhere to the 12- or 12-month amnesty time rule as India and the United States do.

Business process re - engineering patents are the primary area where the patent regimes of the United States, United Kingdom, and India diverge. Patents for business methods have already been issued in the UK and other European nations. In the US, traditional process patents are issued as far as they go beyond simple application of well-known business processes. In India, the economic technique itself cannot be copyrighted, but it may be if it is a novel, methodical approach to solve a technological challenge. The very first novelty and precedence laws of India and the United Kingdom are quite dissimilar from those of the United States. This is the case because novelty and precedence are determined by first time of discovery, not the first time of filing. As a result, the concept of cutting-edge innovation under US patents act becomes complicated.

CHAPTER FIFTEEN

CONCLUSION

In conclusion, we could see that one of the key factors taken into consideration when assessing whether a specific innovation would be patentable or not is novelty. We can also observe the parallels and differences between patent laws practised in India, the United States, and the United Kingdom. Additionally, we can observe in India that an item can indeed be patented just because a known component has taken on a new shape or because a previously unknown use for a specific compound has indeed been identified. An innovation must satisfy the three patentability requirements of novelty, industrial applicability, and original idea in order to be considered patentable.

A worldwide patent for innovations could address the issue of geographical restriction of patents, but in the lack of this patent, each creator must compare the statutory patent frameworks in use in different countries. In order to better understand the patent regimes in use in India, the UK, and the US, this article will outline both their key parallels and distinctions.

The differences in precedent and, to a certain large extend, substantive patent laws and regulations among various nations also impact the lives of the creator. Nevertheless, a closer look at the other side shows that several company goliaths have unfairly benefited from such differences and have therefore patented in a select few nations in order to industrially manipulate their products. In contrast to India, in which a time limit is provided after having to file a detailed specification, the USA heretofore to a first to contrive scheme, and such patents were awarded until an opponent has been created. However, over time, the U.S.A. began to look into its legislation, and lately such privileges have indeed been altered to inventor's 1st right to register.

In conclusion, the primary goal still continues to eliminate the inequality and propose a patent system that is effectiveness in addressing in order to address the shortcomings, improprieties, and gaps in some legal sectors.

The conversation that has just taken place makes it abundantly clear that the Technical Expert Group was correct to advise against

(a) restricting the award of pharmacological material patent applications to new contaminant or healthcare organisations and

(b) with the exception of micro - organisms from patent enrolment due to their potential to violate India's obligations under the TRIPS Agreement. The following components of the TRIPS Agreement justify the Expert Group's suggestion:

The WTO Members are required by Article 27 of the TRIPS Agreement to provide patents "accessible for just any innovation, either goods or methods, in all sectors of innovation, given that such inventions are novel, entail an innovative advance, and are useful for industrial implementation."[1] By refusing to grant patents on innovations that meet the other requirements for patentable subject matter, these exclusion transgress the explicit and comprehensive requirement of TRIPS Article 27.1.

[1]See TRIPS Agreement, supra note 1, art. 27.1 (emphasis added).